A Treasury of Prayers copyright © Frances Lincoln Limited 1996

First published in Great Britain in 1996 by
Frances Lincoln Limited, 4 Torriano Mews
Torriano Avenue, London NW5 2RZ

For photographic acknowledgements and copyright details,
see pages 84-93

With thanks to the Reverend R.C. Paget for his help

British Library Cataloguing in Publication Data
available on request

ISBN 0-7112-1081-0

Set in Footlight MT Light

Printed in Hong Kong
1 3 5 7 9 8 6 4 2

A TREASURY
OF PRAYERS

FRANCES LINCOLN

I said to the man who stood
at the gate of the year:
"Give me a light that I may tread
safely into the unknown."
And he replied:
"Go out into the darkness
and put your hand into the hand
of God. That shall be to you
better than light and safer
than a known way."

Minnie Louise Haskins (1875-1957)

CONTENTS

PRAISING GOD

Praise God, from whom all blessings flow;
Praise him, all creatures here below;
Praise him above ye heavenly host;
Praise Father, Son and Holy Ghost.

Bishop Thomas Ken (1637-1711)

Holy, holy, holy, Lord God of hosts,
heaven and earth are full of thy glory:
Glory be to thee, O Lord most high.

Book of Common Prayer, 1662

Praised be my Lord God with all his creatures, and especially for our brother the sun, who brings us the day and who brings us the light; fair is he and shines with a great splendour; O Lord, he signifies to us thee.

Praised be my Lord for our sister the moon, and for the stars, the which he has set clear and lovely in the heaven.

Praised be my Lord for our sister water, who is very serviceable unto us and humble and precious and clean.

Praised be my Lord for our brother fire, through whom thou givest us light in the darkness; and he is bright and pleasant and very mighty and strong;

Praised be my Lord for our mother the earth, the which doth sustain us and keep us and bringeth forth divers fruits and flowers of many colours and grass.

Praise ye and bless ye the Lord, and give thanks unto him and serve him with great humility.

Canticle of the Creatures
Saint Francis of Assisi (1181-1226)

O God our Father,
we would thank thee for all
the bright things of life. Help us
to see them, and to count them, and
to remember them, that our lives
may flow in ceaseless praise;
for the sake of Jesus Christ our Lord.

Reverend John Henry Jowett (1846-1923)

O Lord, that lends me life,
Lend me a heart replete with thankfulness!

Henry VI, Part 2
William Shakespeare (1564-1616)

Thou that has given so much to me,
Give one thing more, a grateful heart.
Not thankful when it pleases me,
As if thy blessings had spare days;
But such a heart whose very pulse
May be thy praise.

George Herbert (1593-1633)

17

Thanks be to thee, O Lord Jesus Christ, for all the benefits which thou has given us, for all the pains and insults which thou has borne for us. O most merciful Redeemer, friend, and brother, may we know thee more clearly, love thee more dearly, and follow thee more nearly, for thine own sake.

Saint Richard of Chichester (1197-1253)

ASKING FOR FORGIVENESS

Almighty and most merciful Father, we have erred and strayed from thy ways like lost sheep. We have followed too much the devices and desires of our own hearts. We have offended against thy holy laws. We have left undone those things which we ought to have done, and we have done those things which we ought not to have done, and there is no health in us. But thou, O Lord, have mercy upon us miserable offenders. Spare thou them, O God, which confess their faults. Restore thou them that are penitent, according to thy promises declared unto mankind in Christ Jesu our Lord. And grant, O most merciful Father, for his sake, that we may hereafter live a godly, righteous, and sober life, to the glory of thy holy name.

Book of Common Prayer, 1662

O Lord, give us more charity, more self-denial, more likeness to thee. Teach us to sacrifice our comforts to others, and our likings for the sake of doing good. Make us kindly in thought, gentle in word, generous in deed. Teach us that it is better to give than to receive, better to forget ourselves than to put ourselves forward, better to minister than to be ministered unto. And to thee, the God of love, be all glory and praise, now and for ever.

Henry Alford (1810-1871)

O God, who wouldest not the death of a sinner, but that he should be converted and live: forgive the sins of us who turn to thee with all our heart, and grant us the grace of eternal life, through Jesus Christ our Lord.

Early Scottish prayer

We beseech thee, good Lord, that it may please thee to give us true repentance: to forgive us all our sins, negligences, and ignorances; and to endue us with the grace of thy Holy Spirit, to amend our lives according to thy holy word.

Archbishop Cranmer (1489-1556)

WORK AND STUDY

O Lord God, when thou givest to thy servants to endeavour any great matter, grant us also to know that it is not the beginning, but the continuing of the same, until it be thoroughly finished, which yieldeth the true glory; through him that for the finishing of thy work laid down his life, our Redeemer, Jesus Christ.

Sir Francis Drake (1540-1596),
on the day he sailed into Cadiz

Let thy blessing, O Lord, rest upon our work this day. Teach us to seek after truth, and enable us to attain it; but grant that as we increase in the knowledge of earthly things, we may grow in the knowledge of thee, whom to know is life eternal; through Jesus Christ our Lord.

Adapted from Thomas Arnold (1795-1842)

O Lord, never suffer us to think that we can stand by ourselves, and not need thee.

John Donne (1573-1631)

O Heavenly Father, in whom we live and move and have our being, we humbly pray thee so to guide and govern us by thy Holy Spirit, that in all the cares and occupations of our daily life we may never forget thee, but remember that we are ever walking in thy sight; for thine own name's sake.

From an ancient Collect

O Lord, thou knowest how busy I must be this day. If I forget thee, do not thou forget me.

General Lord Astley (1579-1652),
before the battle of Edgehill

FAMILY
AND FRIENDS

O God, the Father of our Lord Jesus Christ, of whom every family in heaven and earth is named, grant unto our friends, to all members of this household, and to all the members of our different families, that, according to the riches of thy glory, we may be strengthened with might by thy spirit in the inner man; that Christ may dwell in our hearts by faith; that we, being rooted and grounded in love, may be able to comprehend with all saints what is the breadth, and length, and depth, and height, and to know the love of Christ which passeth knowledge, that we may be filled with all the fullness of God; through the same Jesus Christ our Lord.

Adapted from the Epistle of Paul the Apostle to the Ephesians, 1st century A.D.

Visit, we beseech thee, most gracious Father, this family and household with thy protection. Let thy blessing descend and rest on all that belong to it, as well absent as present. Grant us and them whatever may be expedient or profitable for our bodies or our souls. Guide us by thy good providence here, and hereafter bring us all to thy glory; through Jesus Christ our Lord.

Reverend Doctor Digby (19th century)

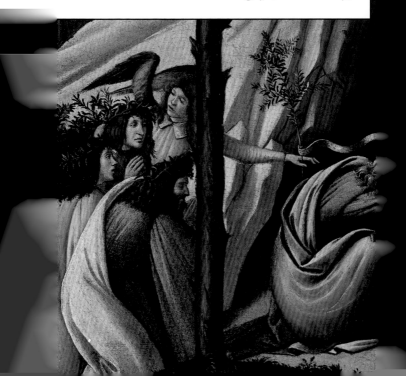

Almighty and most merciful God, who hast given us a new commandment that we should love one another, give us also grace that we may fulfil it. Make us gentle, courteous, and forbearing. Direct our lives so that we may look to the good of others in word and deed. And hallow all our friendships by the blessing of thy spirit; for his sake who loved us and gave himself for us, Jesus Christ our Lord.

Bishop Brooke Foss Westcott (1825-1901)

THE NEEDS
OF THE WORLD

Lord, make me an instrument
of thy peace.
Where there is hatred, let me sow love,
Where there is injury, pardon,
Where there is doubt, faith,
Where there is despair, hope,
Where there is darkness, light,
Where there is sadness, joy.
O divine master, grant that I may not
so much seek to be consoled
as to console, to be understood as
to understand, to be loved as to love;
For it is in giving that we receive,
It is in pardoning that we are
pardoned,
It is in dying that we are born
to eternal life.

Saint Francis of Assisi (1181-1226)

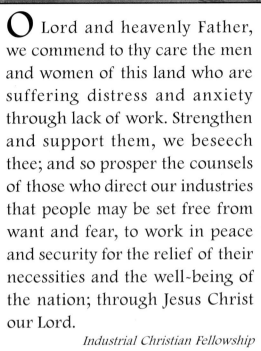

O Lord and heavenly Father, we commend to thy care the men and women of this land who are suffering distress and anxiety through lack of work. Strengthen and support them, we beseech thee; and so prosper the counsels of those who direct our industries that people may be set free from want and fear, to work in peace and security for the relief of their necessities and the well-being of the nation; through Jesus Christ our Lord.

Industrial Christian Fellowship

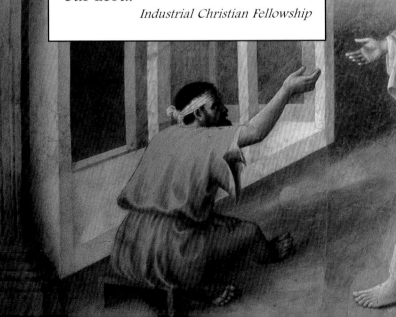

Father, who hast made all men in thy likeness, and lovest all whom thou hast made, suffer not the world to separate itself from thee by building barriers of race and colour.

As thy Son our Saviour was born of a Hebrew mother, yet rejoiced in the faith of a Syrian woman and of a Roman soldier, welcomed the Greeks who sought him and suffered a man from Africa to carry his cross, so teach us to regard the members of all races as fellow-heirs of the kingdom of Jesus Christ our Lord.

Toc H

Hear our humble prayer, O God, for our friends the animals, especially for animals who are suffering; for any that are hunted or lost or deserted or frightened or hungry; for all that must be put to death. We entreat for them all thy mercy and pity and for those who deal with them we ask a heart of compassion, gentle hands and kindly words. Make us ourselves to be true friends to animals and so to share the blessing of the merciful.

Albert Schweitzer (1875-1965)

IN TIME OF TROUBLE

Look in compassion, O heavenly Father, upon this troubled and divided world. Though we cannot trace thy footsteps or understand thy working, give us grace to trust thee with an undoubting faith; and when thine own time is come, reveal, O Lord, that new heaven and new earth wherein dwelleth righteousness, where the Prince of Peace ruleth, thy Son our Saviour Jesus Christ.

Charles John Vaughan (1816-1897)

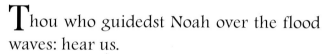

Thou who guidedst Noah over the flood waves: hear us.

Thou who with thy word recalled Jonah from the deep: deliver us.

Thou who stretched forth thy hand to Peter as he sank: help us, O Christ.

Son of God, who didst marvellous things of old: be favourable in our day also.

Early Scottish prayer

Lord, teach me the art of patience whilst I am well, and give me the use of it when I am sick. In that day either lighten my burden or strengthen my back. Make me, who so often in my health have discovered my weakness presuming on my own strength, to be strong in my sickness when I solely rely on thy assistance.

Thomas Fuller (1608-1661)

O God, the Father of lights, from whom cometh down every good and perfect gift: mercifully look upon our frailty and infirmity, and grant us such health of body as thou knowest to be needful for us; that both in body and soul we may evermore serve thee with all our strength; through Jesus Christ our Lord.

John Cosin (1595-1672)

O thou Lord of all worlds, we bless thy name for all those who have entered into their rest, and reached the promised land where thou art seen face to face. Give us grace to follow in their footsteps, as they followed in the footsteps of thy holy Son. Keep alive in us the memory of those dear to ourselves whom thou hast called to thyself; and grant that every remembrance which turns our hearts from things seen to things unseen may lead us always upwards to thee, till we come to our eternal rest; through Jesus Christ our Lord.

Fenton John Anthony Hort (1828-1892)

May God be with me and with his messenger whom he has sent to greet me and lead me to heaven.

May the Lord who is great and blessed look upon me, have pity on me and grant me peace. May he give me greater strength and courage that I may not be fearful or afraid.

For the angels of God are about me and God is with me wherever I may be.

Jewish prayer

PRAYERS FOR EVERY DAY

Our Father, which art in heaven,
Hallowed be thy name,
Thy kingdom come,
Thy will be done,
in earth as it is in heaven.
Give us this day our daily bread.
And forgive us our trespasses,
As we forgive them that trespass
against us;
And lead us not into temptation;
But deliver us from evil:
For thine is the kingdom,
the power and the glory,
For ever and ever.

Book of Common Prayer, 1662

Lord, give us faith that right makes might.

Abraham Lincoln (1809-1865)

Take from us, O God, all pride and vanity, all boasting and forwardness, and give us the true courage that shows itself by gentleness; the true wisdom that shows itself by simplicity; and the true power that shows itself by modesty; through Jesus Christ our Lord.

Charles Kingsley (1819-1875)

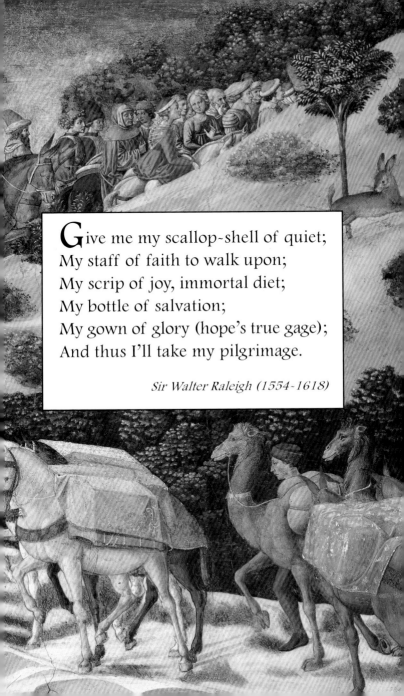

Give me my scallop-shell of quiet;
My staff of faith to walk upon;
My scrip of joy, immortal diet;
My bottle of salvation;
My gown of glory (hope's true gage);
And thus I'll take my pilgrimage.

Sir Walter Raleigh (1554-1618)

God be in my head,
and in my understanding;
God be in my eyes,
and in my looking;
God be in my mouth,
and in my speaking;
God be in my heart,
and in my thinking;
God be at my end,
and at my departing.

16th-century Sarum Primer

God, give us the serenity to accept
what cannot be changed;
Give us the courage to change what
should be changed;
Give us the wisdom to distinguish one
from the other.

Reinhold Niebuhr (1892-1971)

O Gracious and holy Father
Give us wisdom to perceive thee,
intelligence to understand thee,
diligence to seek thee,
patience to wait for thee,
eyes to behold thee,
a heart to meditate upon thee,
and a life to proclaim thee;
through the power of the spirit
of Jesus Christ our Lord.

Saint Benedict (480-c.550)

Give me, good Lord, a full faith,
a firm hope and a fervent charity,
a love to thee incomparable above
the love to myself.

*Saint Thomas More (1478-1535),
from a prayer written before his execution*

Incline us O God! to think humbly of ourselves, to be saved only in the examination of our own conduct, to consider our fellow-creatures with kindness, and to judge of all they say and do with the charity which we would desire from them ourselves.

Jane Austen (1775-1817)

Christ be with me, Christ before me,
Christ behind me,
Christ in me, Christ beneath me,
Christ above me,
Christ on my right, Christ on my left,
Christ where I lie, Christ where I sit,
Christ where I arise,
Christ in the heart of every one
who thinks of me,
Christ in the mouth of every one
who speaks of me,
Christ in every eye that sees me,
Christ in every ear that hears me.
Salvation is of the Lord!
May thy salvation, O Lord,
be ever with us.

The Breastplate of Saint Patrick (c.373-463)

Teach us, good Lord, to serve thee
as thou deservest,
to give and not to count the cost;
to fight and not to heed the wounds;
to toil and not to seek for rest;
to labour and not to ask for any reward
save that of knowing that we do thy will.

Saint Ignatius Loyola (1491-1556)

GRACE BEFORE MEALS

Heavenly Father, make us thankful
to thee and mindful of others as we
receive these blessings, in Jesus' name.

The Book of Common Worship

Be present at our table, Lord,
Be here and everywhere adored:
Thy creatures bless, and grant that we
May feast in paradise with thee.

John Cennick (1718-1755)

O Lord who fed the multitudes with
five barley loaves, bless what we are
about to eat.

Egyptian Arabic grace

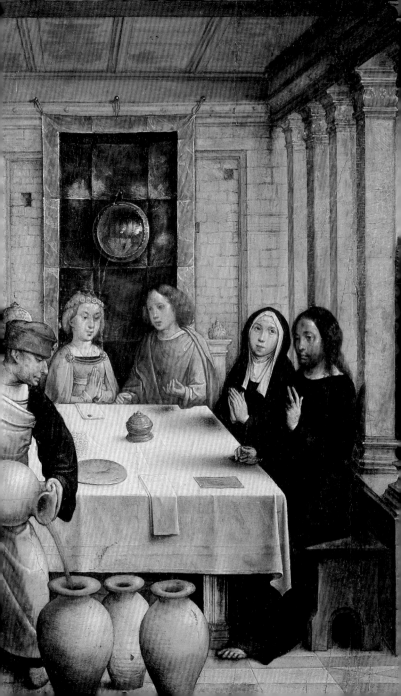

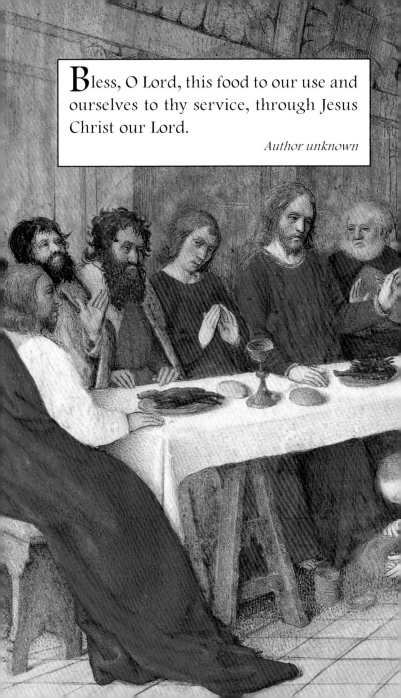

Bless, O Lord, this food to our use and ourselves to thy service, through Jesus Christ our Lord.

Author unknown

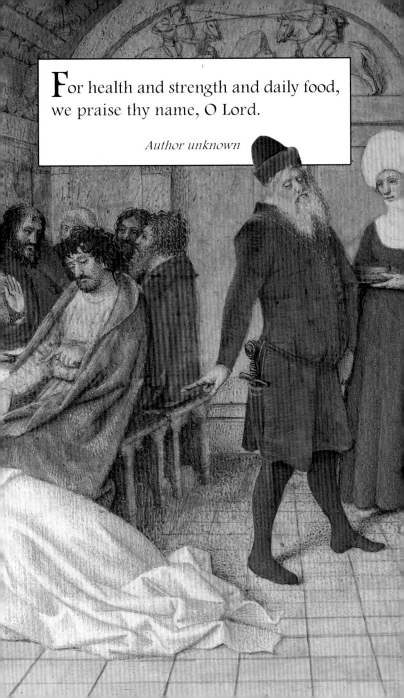

For health and strength and daily food,
we praise thy name, O Lord.

Author unknown

Morning and Evening

O Lord our heavenly Father, almighty and everlasting God, who hast safely brought us to the beginning of this day: defend us in the same with thy mighty power; and grant that this day we fall into no sin, neither run into any kind of danger; but that all our doings may be ordered by thy governance, to do always that is righteous in thy sight; through Jesus Christ our Lord.

Book of Common Prayer, 1662

Here, Lord, is my life. I place it on the altar today. Use it as you will.

Albert Schweitzer (1875-1965)

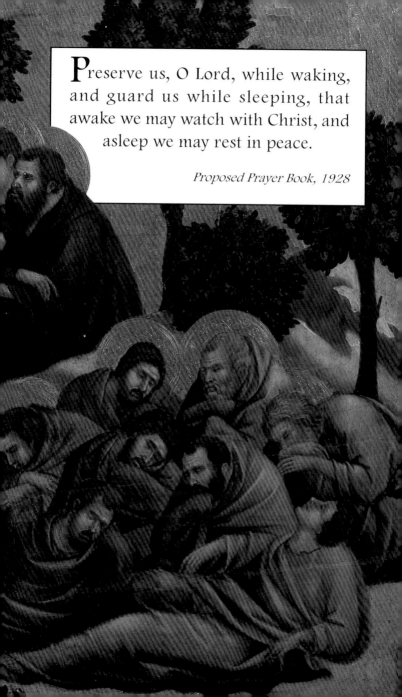

Preserve us, O Lord, while waking, and guard us while sleeping, that awake we may watch with Christ, and asleep we may rest in peace.

Proposed Prayer Book, 1928

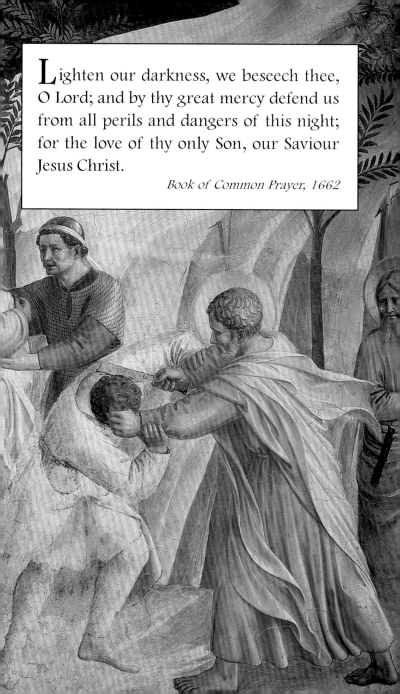

Lighten our darkness, we beseech thee, O Lord; and by thy great mercy defend us from all perils and dangers of this night; for the love of thy only Son, our Saviour Jesus Christ.

Book of Common Prayer, 1662

Go forth into the world in peace;
be of good courage;
hold fast that which is good;
render to no man evil for evil;
strengthen the fainthearted;
support the weak;
help the afflicted;
honour all men;
love and serve the Lord, rejoicing
in the power of the Holy Spirit.

And the blessing of God Almighty,
the Father, the Son and the Holy
Ghost, be upon you, and remain
with you for ever.

Proposed Prayer Book, 1928

Index of Artists and Paintings

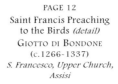

PAGES 14-15
The Annunciation *(detail)* Fresco
FRA ANGELICO (c.1395-1455)
Museo di S. Marco, Florence

PAGE 16
The Young Cicero Reading *(detail)* Fresco
VINCENZO FOPPA (active 1456-c.1515)
Wallace Collection, London

PAGE 17
Portrait of an Old Man
(detail)
FILIPPINO LIPPI
(c.1457-1504)
*Galleria degli Uffizi,
Florence*

PAGE 18
The Dead Christ
supported by Two Angels
(detail)
CARLO CRIVELLI
(c.1430/5-c.1494)
The National Gallery, London

PAGE 19
Mary Magdalen
(detail)
The Braque Family Triptych
ROGIER VAN DER WEYDEN
(c.1399-1464)
Louvre, Paris

PAGE 20
Adam and Eve
banished from Paradise
(detail)
RAMON DE MURE
(active 1412-1435)
*Museu Episcopal,
Vic*

PAGES 22-23
Christ Washing
the Disciples' Feet
(detail)
DUCCIO DI BUONINSEGNA
(active 1278-c.1319)
*Museo dell'Opera
del Duomo, Siena*

PAGE 24
Christ in the House of
Martha and Mary
(detail)
JAN VERMEER
(1632-1675)
*National Gallery of Scotland,
Edinburgh*

PAGE 25
The Tribute Money
TITIAN
(active c.1506; died 1576)
The National Gallery,
London

PAGE 26
Saint Jerome in his Study
(detail)
DOMENICO GHIRLANDAIO
(1449-1494)
Galleria degli Uffizi, Florence

PAGE 27
Crucifixion *(detail)*
PIETRO PERUGINO
(living 1469; died1523)
Church of S. Agostino,
Siena

PAGE 28
A Girl Writing
(detail)
NETHERLANDISH SCHOOL
(c.1520)
The National Gallery,
London

PAGE 29
Saint Christopher
MASTER OF THE
EMBROIDERED FOLIAGE
(active c.1500)
Gemäldegalerie
Alte Meister, Dresden

PAGES 30-31
Saint Eloi in the Silversmith's
Workshop *(detail)*
TADDEO GADDI (c.1300-1366)
Prado, Madrid

PAGE 32
The Scullery Maid
(detail)
GIUSEPPE MARIA CRESPI
(1665-1747)
Fondazione
Contini Bonacossi,
Florence

PAGE 33
Saint Joseph, the Carpenter *(detail)*
GEORGES DE LA TOUR (1593-1652)
Louvre, Paris

PAGE 34
The Holy Family with
Saints Elizabeth
and John *(detail)*
After NICHOLAS POUSSIN
(after 1640)
The National Gallery,
London

PAGES 36-38
'Mystic Nativity' *(details)*
SANDRO BOTTICELLI (c.1445-1510)
The National Gallery, London

PAGE 40
The Conversion of
Saint Hubert *(detail)*
Workshop of the
MASTER OF THE LIFE
OF THE VIRGIN
(c.1480/85)
The National Gallery,
London

PAGES 42-43
Saint Peter Healing a Cripple *(detail)* Fresco
MASOLINO (c.1383-after 1432)
Brancacci Chapel, Santa Maria del Carmine,
Florence

PAGE 44
The Adoration of the Magi
(detail)
HUGO VAN DER GOES
(active 1467; died 1482)
Hermitage, St Petersburg

PAGE 47
Saint Giles and the Hind
(detail)
MASTER OF SAINT GILES,
(active c.1500)
The National Gallery,
London

PAGE 48
Saint John leading home
his Adopted Mother
(detail)
WILLIAM DYCE (1806-1864)
Forbes Magazine Collection,
London

PAGES 50-51
Miraculous Draught of Fishes
(detail)
KONRAD WITZ (1400/10-1444/6)
Musée d'Art et d'Histoire, Geneva

PAGE 52
Saint Lawrence
distributing alms *(detail)*
FRA ANGELICO (c.1395-1455)
*Chapel of Nicholas V,
Vatican, Rome*

PAGE 54
The Blind of Jericho, or Christ
Healing the Blind *(detail)*
NICHOLAS POUSSIN (1594-1665)
Louvre, Paris

PAGE 55
Seven Saints
FRA FILIPPO LIPPI (c.1406-1469)
The National Gallery, London

PAGE 57
Tobias and the Angel
(detail)
Attrib. ANDREA DEL VERROCCHIO
(c.1435-1488)
The National Gallery, London

PAGE 58
Agony in the Garden
(detail)
SANDRO BOTTICELLI
(c.1445-1510)
Capilla Real, Granada

PAGE 60
Saint Michael *(detail)*
BERNADINO ZENALE
(1436-1526)
*Galleria degli Uffizi,
Florence*

PAGE 61
Saint Catherine *(detail)*
After BERNARDINO LUINI
(active 1512; died 1532)
The National Gallery, London

PAGES 62-63
Journey of the Magi
(detail) Fresco
BENOZZO GOZZOLI
(c.1421-1497)
*Palazzo Medici-Riccardi,
Florence*

PAGE 64
Head of a Saint *(detail)*
VENEZIANO DOMENICO
(active 1438; died 1461)
*The National Gallery,
London*

PAGE 65
The Trinity *(detail)*
J. BACO (1410-1461) and
J. REXACH (1415-1484)
Musée de Picardie, Amiens

PAGE 66
Noli me tangere
FRA ANGELICO
(c.1395-1455)
*Museo di S. Marco,
Florence*

PAGE 67
Resurrection *(detail)*
PIERO DELLA FRANCESCA
(1410/20-1492)
*Pinacoteca Comunale,
Sansepolcro*

PAGE 69
The Charity of
Saint Lucy *(detail)*
JACOBELLO DEL FIORE
(died 1439)
Pinacoteca Civica, Fermo

PAGE 70
Baptism of Christ
(detail)
Workshop of
BICCI DI LORENZO (1375-1452)
York City Art Gallery

PAGE 71
Saint George and
the Dragon *(detail)* Icon
SYRIAN
Early period (c.800)

PAGE 73
The Marriage Feast
at Cana *(detail)*
JUAN DE FLANDRES
(active from 1496;
died before 1519)
Private Collection

PAGES 74-75
Mary Magdalen
washing Christ's feet
(detail)
The Hours of Etienne Chevalier
JEAN FOUQUET (c.1425-c.1480)
Musée Condé, Chantilly

PAGE 76
Holy Family with
a Palm Tree
Tondo
RAPHAEL (1483-1520)
*Duke of Sutherland
Collection, on loan to
the National Gallery of
Scotland, Edinburgh*

PAGE 77
The Annunciation
(detail)
Panel from
the Main Altarpiece
JUAN DE FLANDRES
(active from 1496;
died before 1519)
*Palencia Cathedral,
Palencia*

PAGES 78-79
Agony in the Garden
of Gethsemene
(detail)
DUCCIO DI BUONINSEGNA
(active 1278-c.1319)
*Museo dell'Opera
del Duomo, Siena*

PAGES 80-81
The Arrest of Jesus *(detail)*
FRA ANGELICO (c.1395-1455)
*Museo di San Marco
dell'Angelico, Florence*

PAGE 82
God the Father Enthroned
(detail)
Polyptych of the Apocalypse
JACOPO ALBEREGNO
(died 1397)
*Galleria dell'Accademia,
Venice*

BACK JACKET
The Virgin in a Rose Arbour *(detail)*
STEPHAN LOCHNER (active 1442-1451)
Wallraf-Richartz Museum, Cologne

Index of First Lines

Photographic Acknowledgements

For permission to reproduce the paintings on the following pages and for supplying photographs, the Publishers thank:

Bridgeman Art Library, London: Endpapers, 9, 10-11, 12, 16, 17, 19, 20, 22-23, 24, 26, 27, 30-31, 42-43, 44, 48, 50-51, 52, 58, 60, 62-63, 69, 70, 74-75, 76, 78-79, 80-81, 82, back jacket

Christie's London/Bridgeman Art Library, London: 73

Gemäldegalerie Alte Meister, Dresden: 29

Giraudon/Bridgeman Art Library, London: 33, 54, 65

Index/Bridgeman Art Library, London: 77

The National Gallery, London: front jacket, 6, 8, 18, 25, 28, 34, 36-37, 38, 40, 47, 55, 57, 61, 64

Richardson and Kailas Icons, London/Bridgeman Art Library, London: 71

The Royal Collection © 1996 Her Majesty Queen Elizabeth II: 5

Scala, Florence: 14-15, 32, 66, 67

Acknowledgements

The publishers would like to thank the following for permission to reprint copyright material:

Cambridge University Press for extracts from the Authorized King James Version of *The Book of Common Prayer,* 1662, the rights in which are vested in the Crown and reproduced by permission of the Crown's Patentee, Cambridge University Press; the Central Board of Finance of the Church of England for prayers from *The Prayer Book as Proposed in 1928*; Franciscan Herald Press for extracts from *St Francis of Assisi Omnibus of Sources: Early Writings and Early Biographies,* edited by Marion A. Habis OFM, 1973; the estate of Minnie Louise Haskins for the extract from *The Gate of The Year* by Minnie Louise Haskins (Hodder & Stoughton, 1940); the Industry Churches Forum for the prayer of the Industrial Christian Fellowship; Rhena Schweitzer-Miller and the Albert Schweitzer Fellowship for two prayers by Albert Schweitzer; and Toc H for the prayer from *A Pocketful of Prayers*, 1931.

All efforts have been made to trace any other copyright holders but without success. The publishers will be pleased to rectify any omissions in future editions.